THE NATURE KIDS GUIDE TO
TASMANIAN DEVILS

DAVID ANDERSON

LP Media Inc. Publishing
Text copyright © 2026 by LP Media Inc.
All rights reserved.

For information address LP Media Inc. Publishing,
30012 Variolite St NW, Princeton MN 55371
www.lpmedia.org

Publication Data

Tasmanian Devils
The Nature Kid's Guide to Tasmanian Devils — First edition.

Summary: "Learn all about Tasmanian Devils, the Nature Kid Way"
— Provided by publisher.

ISBN: 979-8-89818-135-2

[1. Tasmanian Devils – Non-Fiction] I. Title.

Title: The Nature Kid's Guide to Tasmanian Devils

CONTENTS

DARK DENS

DID YOU KNOW?

Tasmania is about the same size as West Virginia. The island has mountains, rainforests, and beaches. Devils can live in almost any habitat there!

Snarl! A black shape runs into a hollow log. A Tasmanian devil peeks out of its home.

Tasmanian Devils make homes in many different habitats. They live in dry forests as well as coastal areas near the beach. They live in open grasslands and even on farmland.

Devils like forests that are open and not too thick. This makes it easier for them to travel long distances at night while looking for food. They can walk up to 10 miles in a single night!

A good den is the most important thing a devil needs. During the day, they sleep in hollow logs, rocky caves, thick bushes, or old wombat burrows

ISLAND ONLY

Growl! A devil sniffs the cool night air. It roams its island home.

Tasmanian devils live wild only in Tasmania. This island is south of mainland Australia.

Long ago, devils lived on the mainland Australia too. They left about 3,000 years ago.

Wild dogs called dingoes pushed them out. People pushed them out. Weather changes pushed them out too. Dingoes never got to Tasmania. So devils stayed safe there.

Tasmania is about 150 miles south of Australia. It's about a 1 hour flight from the mainland.

SMALL BUT SCRAPPY

A devil stands looks around the forest. He's small but fearless.

Tasmanian devils are the size of a small dog like a Chihuahua or Pomeranian. They weigh between 9 and 26 pounds. Males are bigger than females.

Devils stand about 12 inches tall at the shoulder. Their bodies stretch 20 to 31 inches long. Their tails add another 9 to 12 inches.

Although they are small, they are the largest meat-eating marsupials in the world.

A devil's head is very large for its body. This helps it bite with great force.

BONE CRUSHERS

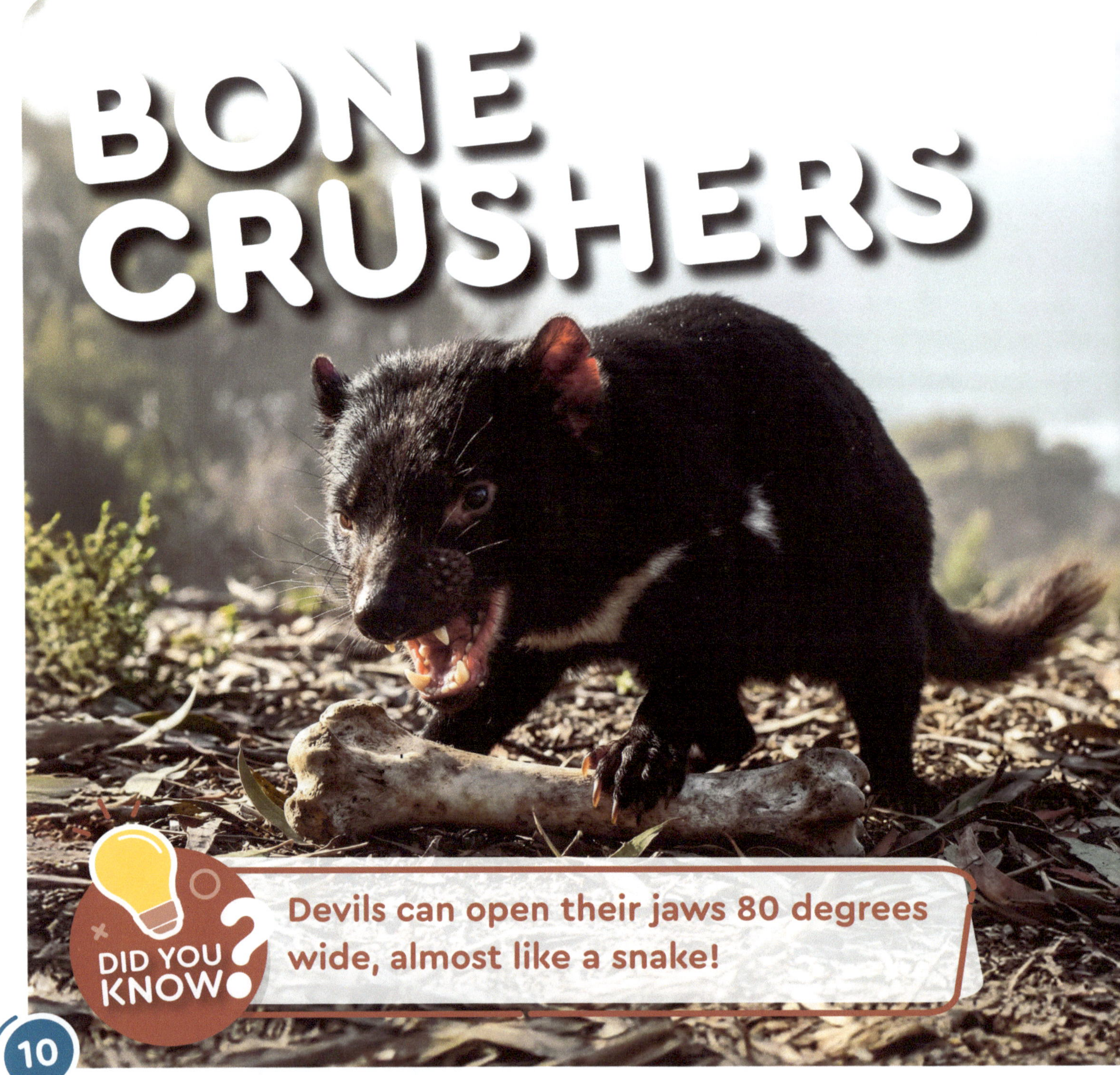

Crunch! A devil bites through a thick bone. Its jaws are so strong!

Tasmanian devils have very powerful jaws. They can bite through thick bones with ease. Their bite is one of the strongest of any mammal for their size.

Devils have 42 sharp teeth. Their back teeth work like scissors, slicing through tough meat and skin.

Their front teeth are made for gripping and tearing food apart. Devils also have jaw muscles that attach high on their skull. This gives them extra biting power.

SNIFF IT

Sniff! A devil lifts its nose high. It smells food far away.

Tasmanian devils have an amazing sense of smell. They can sniff out dead animals from half a mile away. Their long whiskers help them feel around in the dark.

Devils have good hearing too. Their big ears catch soft sounds at night.

Their eyesight is not as strong. They see moving things better than still ones.

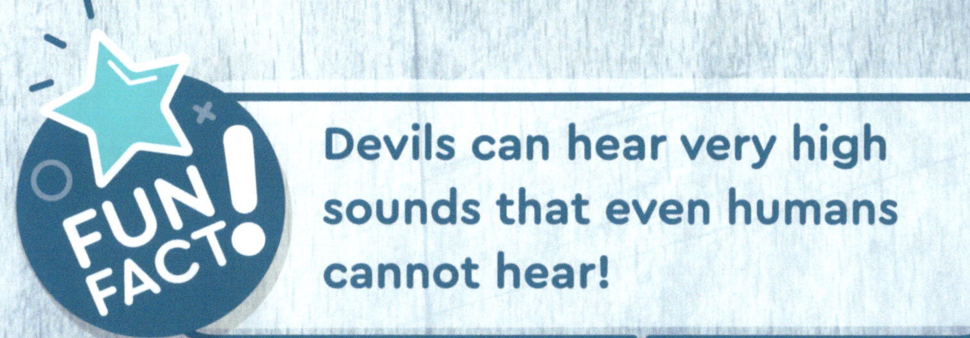

SCARY
SCREAMS

Screech! A devil opens its mouth wide. It screams loud!

Tasmanian devils make scary sounds. They do this to stay safe. They screech. They growl. They scream. These loud sounds scare other animals away.

Devils open their mouths very wide. This shows their sharp teeth. It makes them look fierce.

Their ears turn bright red when upset. This tells others to stay back.

A devil's scream is very loud. You can hear it from a mile away at night.

MESSY MEALS

Chomp! A devil swallows a large chunk of meat. He almost chokes!

Tasmanian devils are messy eaters. They eat almost every part of an animal. They eat meat, fur, and bones. They even eat organs.

Devils are **scavengers**. This means they eat animals that are already dead. They use their strong sense of smell to find dead animals.

A devil can eat a lot in one meal. It can eat 40 percent of its body weight! That would be like you eating 100 hamburgers at once!

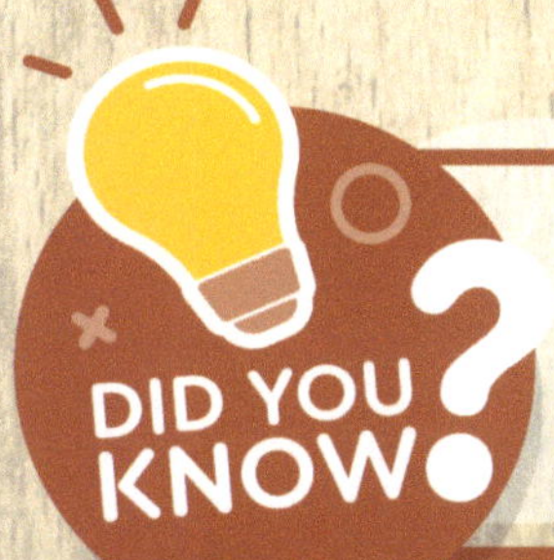

Devils can digest bones, teeth, and even hooves!

CHOMP DOWN

Devils eat so fast that a group can finish a whole wallaby in just 15 minutes!

Snap! A devil clamps down on a bone. The bone splinters and breaks.

Tasmanian devils have a special way of eating. They bite down and twist their whole body. This ripping motion tears meat off bones.

Devils do not chew their food much. They gulp down big chunks instead. Their strong stomach acid breaks down everything they swallow.

When many devils find the same carcass, they eat together. They push and shove to get the best spots. All this fighting fills the air with loud screaming.

Devils use their front paws to hold food steady. Then they pull and tear with their powerful jaws.

WATCH OUT

Swoosh! A big eagle dives down. The devil runs fast!

Tasmanian devils do not have many predators. They are the biggest meat-eating marsupials on their island. These fierce animals can scare away threats.

Young devils face more danger. Wedge-tailed eagles swoop down. They hunt baby devils. Big snakes can also hurt them.

Grown-up devils are tough to attack. Their loud screams scare enemies. Their strong bites keep predators away.

Wedge-tailed eagles have wings up to 9 feet wide. They spot prey from high above!

HIDE FAST

Rustle! A devil squeezes into a log and hides in the dark.

Tasmanian devils have many ways to stay safe. They squeeze into tight spaces. Hollow logs and rock cracks make good hiding spots.

Devils can climb trees when they need to escape. Young devils climb better than adults. Their sharp claws help them grip the bark.

Devils also run into their dens to hide when they sense danger is near.

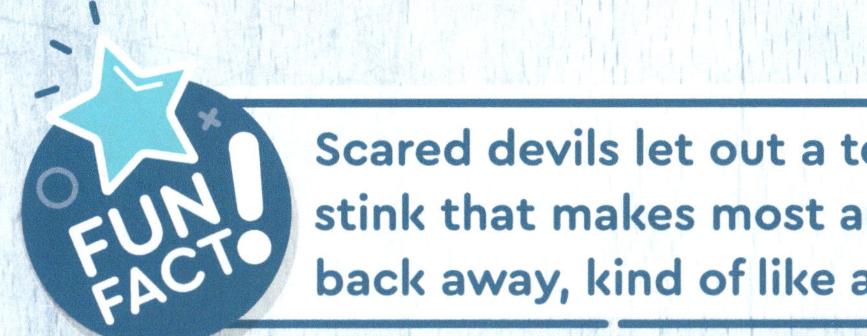

DASH
DEVILS
24

Stomp! A devil runs through the brush. Its short legs move fast!

Tasmanian devils are not very fast runners. They can run up to 15 miles per hour in short bursts. They use this speed to chase prey or escape danger.

Devils have a clumsy-looking walk. They waddle from side to side. Their short legs make them look funny when they move.

But devils can travel far! They will walk up to 10 miles in one night looking for food.

Baby devils are great climbers. Adults are too heavy, so they stay on the ground.

NIGHT SHIFT

Hoot! The sun goes down. A devil wakes up and stretches.

Tasmanian devils are **nocturnal**. This means they are active at night. They sleep during the day in their dens.

When darkness falls, devils come out to search for food. Their excellent sense of smell helps them find meals in the dark.

Devils spend most of the night moving around. Then they return to their dens before sunrise.

Tasmanian devils yawn to show fear, not because they are tired. They open wide to scare enemies!

LONER LIFE

Snap! A devil walks alone through the forest. Night is almost here.

Tasmanian devils live alone most of the time. They do not form packs or families. Each devil has its own **territory**.

Devils usually come together only to eat and to mate. Many devils may share a large meal. But they growl and scream at each other while eating.

After eating, each devil goes its own way.

A devil's home range can cover up to 13 square miles. That is a lot of land!

MATING
SEASON

Sniff! A male follows a scent trail, he's looking for a female.

Tasmanian devils have one mating season each year in March. During this time, females are ready to mate for about three weeks.

Males travel far to find females. They follow scent trails through the forest. These trails can lead many males to the same female.

Males often fight over females. They bite and scratch each other. The strongest male usually wins.

A female devil can mate with more than one male. Her babies may have different fathers!

TINY JOEYS

Chirp! Four young devils play outside their den. They have grown up fast!

Baby Tasmanian devils are called joeys. These tiny babies are born after just 21 days. A newborn joey is only the size of a grain of rice!

A mother can have up to 30 babies at once. But her pouch only has room for four. The first four joeys to reach the pouch will grow up there.

Joeys stay in the pouch for about four months. They grow fur and open their eyes. Then they ride on their mother's back.

Joeys are born without ears or back legs. These body parts grow while they are safe inside the pouch!

POUCH POWER

A mother devil curls up in her den. Tiny joey are growing in her pouch.

Tasmanian devils are **marsupials**. This means mothers carry babies in a pouch. The pouch keeps joeys safe and warm.

Joeys stay attached to a nipple inside the pouch for about 100 days. The milk they drink contains special proteins that help them fight germs.

When joeys leave the pouch, they still need their mother. She keeps them in a den for about four more months. Then, at about nine months old, young devils leave their mother.

A mother devil's pouch opens toward her tail, not her head!

DEADLY DISEASE

Snort! A sick devil has bumps on its face. These bumps make it hard to eat.

Many Tasmanian devils are sick. They have a disease called Devil Facial Tumor Disease. It spreads when devils bite each other.

This disease causes lumps on their faces. The lumps grow big and stop devils from eating.

Scientists work hard to help. They keep healthy devils safe on islands and in zoos.

This disease was first seen in 1996. It has killed about 80 percent of wild devils.

HELPING HANDS

Grunt! A healthy devil sniffs the air, he lives in a devil sanctuary.

People help Tasmanian devils. Scientists catch healthy devils. They move them to safe places. Some go to islands. These islands have no disease.

Zoos around the world raise healthy devils. They help devils have babies.

Some devils can now fight the disease. Their bodies are getting stronger. Devils will survive and thrive!

FUN FACT!

Over 700 healthy Tasmanian devils live in breeding programs around the world.

GLOSSARY

marsupials
Animals that carry their babies in a pouch on their belly.

scavengers
Animals that eat other animals that are already dead.

nocturnal
Awake and active at night instead of during the day.

sanctuary
A safe place where animals are protected from harm.

territory
An area of land that an animal lives in and protects as its own.